WEEKLY READER BOOKS presents

What Is the Moon?

A **Just Ask**™ Book

Hi, my name is Christopher!

by Chris Arvetis
and Carole Palmer

illustrated by
James Buckley

FIELD PUBLICATIONS
MIDDLETOWN, CT.

Look at the big bright circle in the sky.

Why, that's the moon!

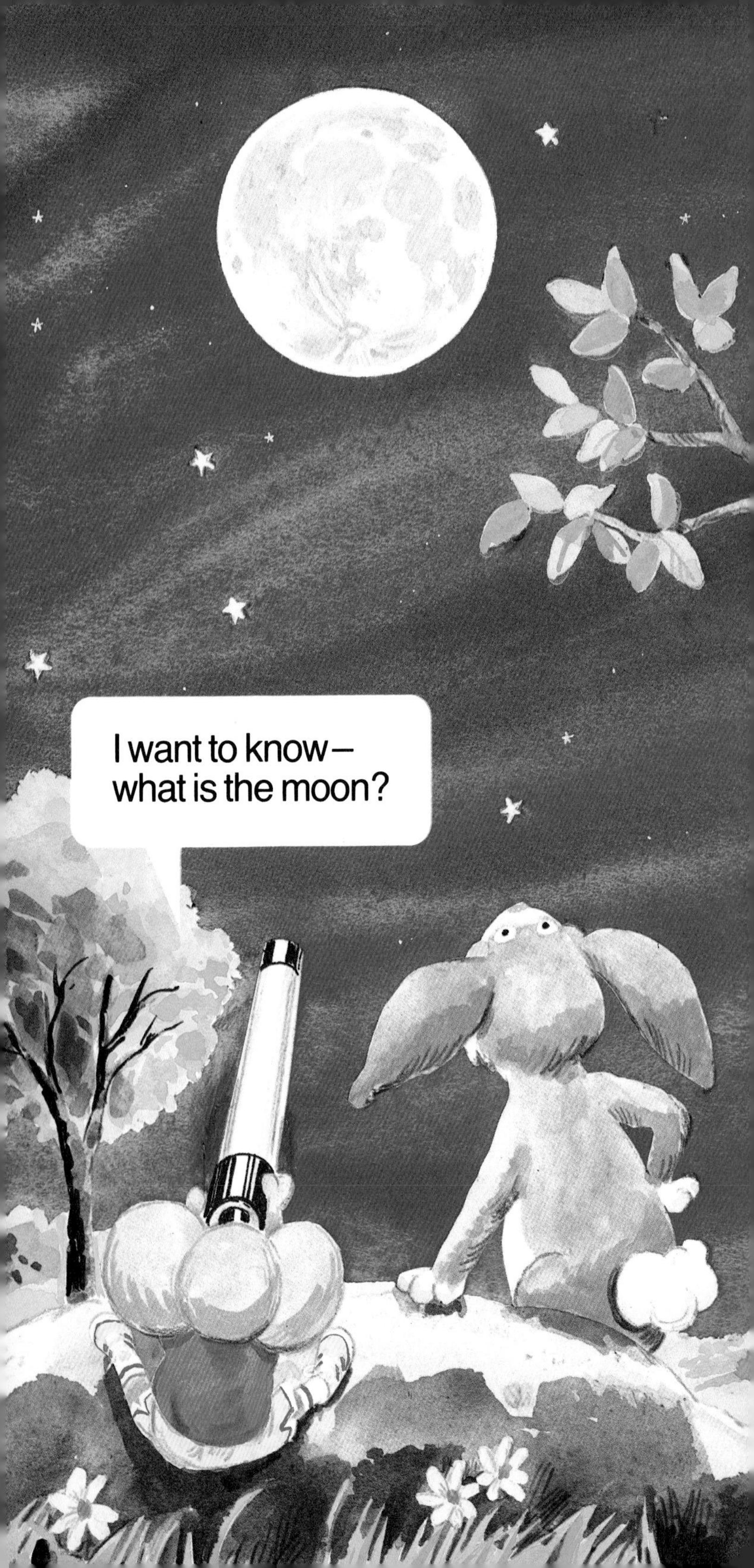
I want to know–
what is the moon?

Well, the moon is a huge ball of rock. It lights up the sky at night.

The moon looks like a round, gray ball with some darker gray patches.
These dark gray patches are flat land.

Look at my picture.
The rest of the moon is rough.
It has big mountains.
These parts are called highlands.

The large dents that look like bowls are called craters.
That's CRA-TERS!

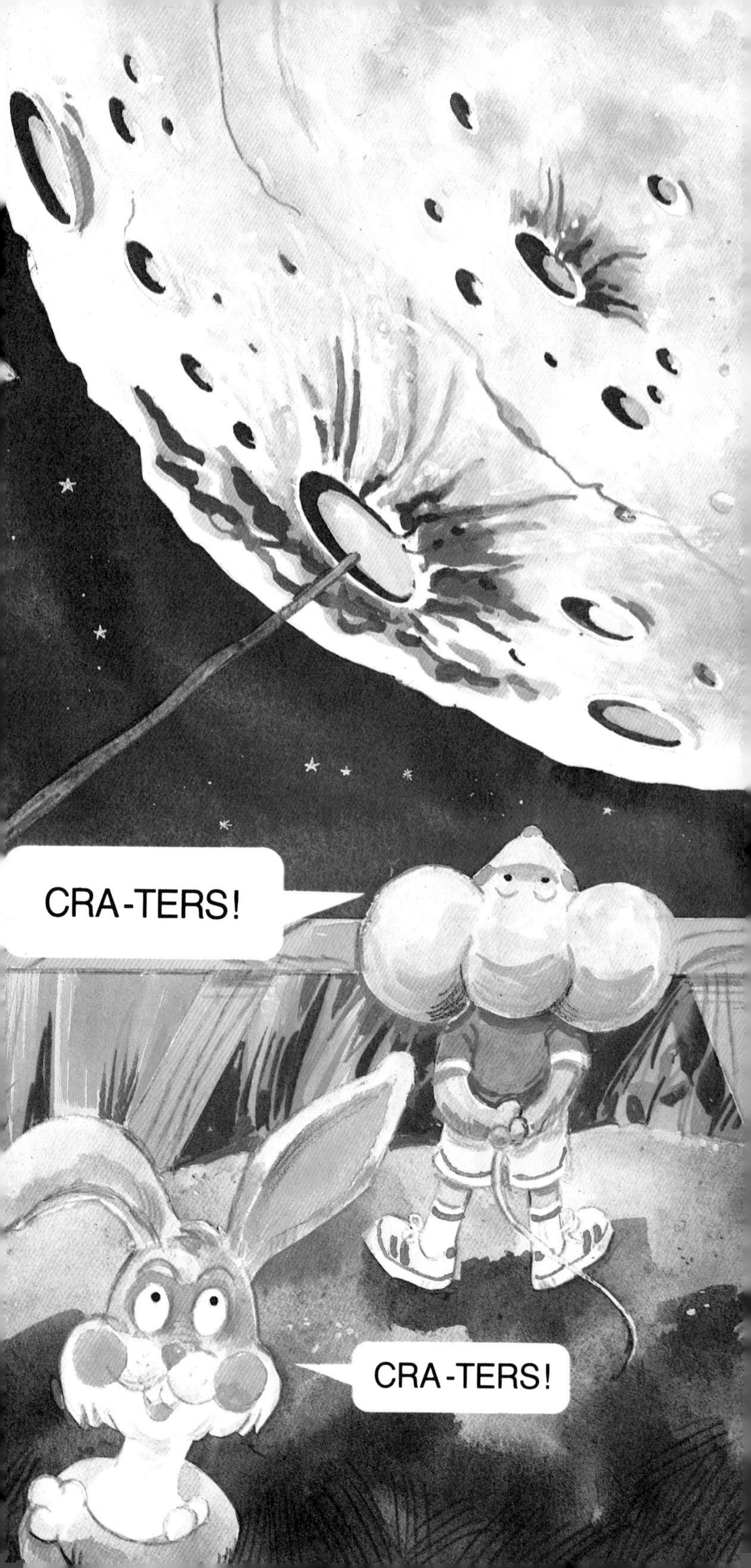
CRA-TERS!
CRA-TERS!

The craters are made when hard things hit the moon. Some of the craters look like volcanoes.

You have big eyes!

The moon has valleys, too. The long narrow ones look like big cracks in the moon.

There are also winding valleys that look like dried-up rivers.

The moon goes around the earth.
It follows a path like this.
It takes about a month
to make one trip.

Astronauts have traveled to the moon. They have walked on the moon. Since then, we know a lot more about the moon.

We know that it is very quiet and lonely on the moon. There are no plants, animals, or people.

There is no air or wind on the moon.
You could not fly a kite on the moon.

There is no water.
The temperature is a lot hotter and colder than anywhere on earth.

You would have to wear a spacesuit if you traveled to the moon.
You would be much lighter on the moon.
You would float in space and bounce as you walk.
Like this?

As people study about the moon, we will know more about it.
Some day, the moon may be a space station for space travelers.

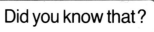

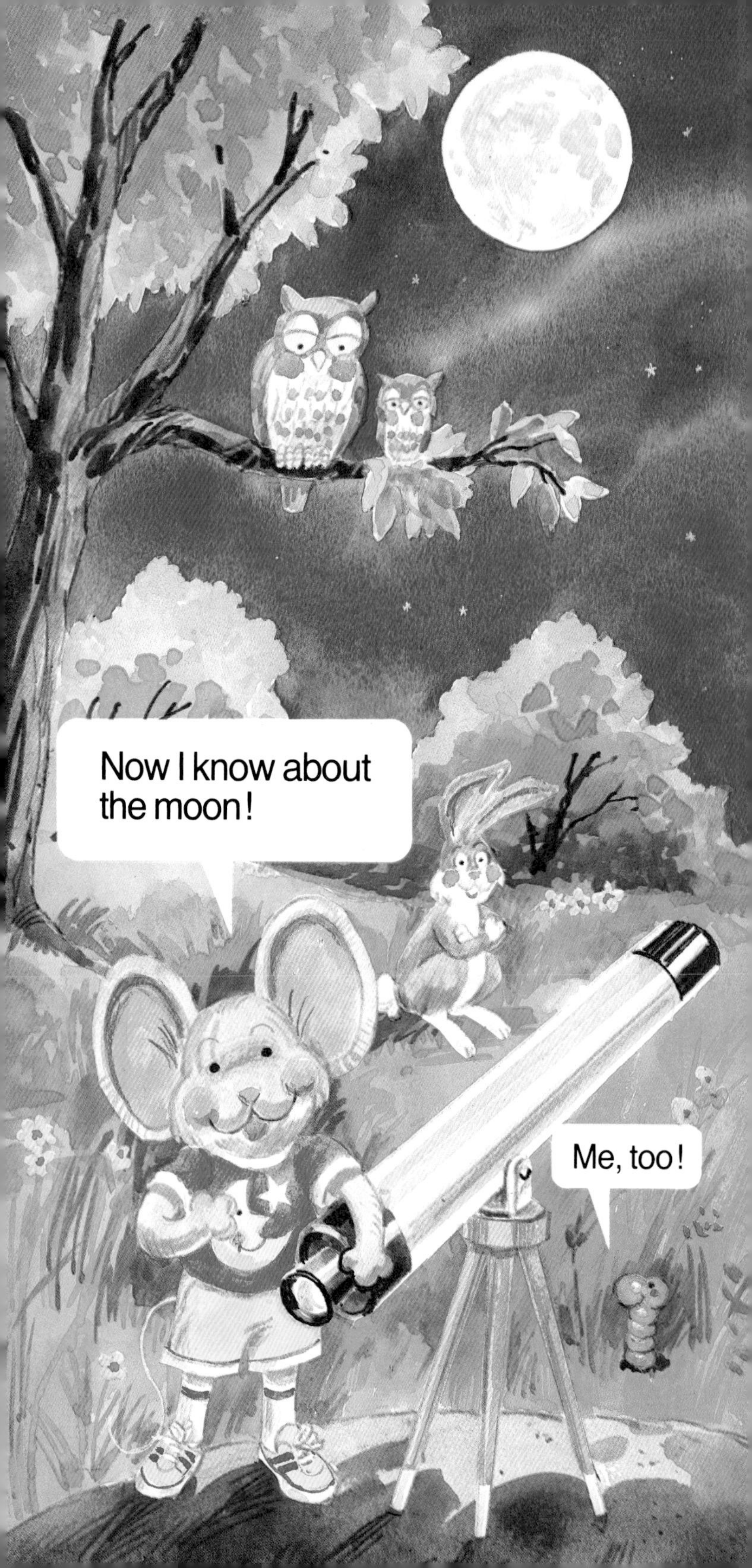
Now I know about the moon!
Me, too!